THE

CLASSICAL GUITAR LIBRARY

Volume II

Transcribed by JERRY SNYDER

• Bach • Bartok • Beethoven • Handel •
• Mozart • Scarlatti •

Cover: Quintern Player by Tobias Simmer: woodcut, 1580.
Print courtesy of The New York Public Library.
The Special Collections Print and Photographs Division.

— CONTENTS —

JOHANN SEBASTIAN BACH

BÉLA BARTÓK

LUDWIG VAN BEETHOVEN

GEORGE FRIDERIC HANDEL

WOLFGANG AMADEUS MOZART

DOMENICO SCARLATTI

MENUET

JOHANN SEBASTIAN BACH (1685-1750)
From Anna Magdalena No. 2, Anh. 114
Transcribed by JERRY SNYDER

AIR ON THE G STRING

JOHANN SEBASTIAN BACH (1685-1750)
from Orchestra Suite No. 3, BWV 1068
Transcribed by JERRY SNYDER

CHORALE

JOHANN SEBASTIAN BACH (1685-1750)
Transcribed by JERRY SNYDER

BE THOU WITH ME

(Bist Du Bei Mir)

JOHANN SEBASTIAN BACH (1685-1750)
from Anna Magdalena Notebook, BWV 508
Transcribed by JERRY SNYDER

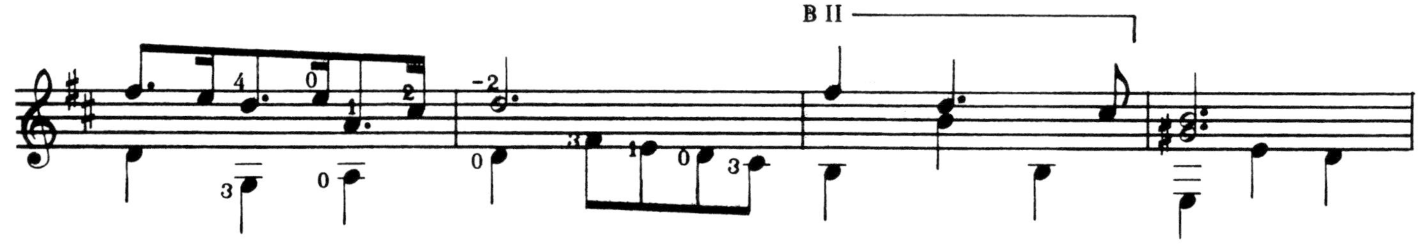

B II
B II

ALLEGRETTO

BÉLA BARTÓK (1881-1945)
from For Children
Transcribed by JERRY SNYDER

ANDANTE

BÉLA BARTÓK (1881-1945)
from For Children
Transcribed by JERRY SNYDER

BALLAD

BÉLA BARTÓK (1881-1945)
from For Children
Transcribed by JERRY SNYDER

DIALOGUE

BÉLA BARTÓK (1881-1945)
from The First Term At The Piano
Transcribed by JERRY SNYDER

Moderato

f

PEASANT'S DANCE

BÉLA BARTÓK (1881-1945)
from The First Term At The Piano
Transcribed by JERRY SNYDER

Allegro moderato

FOLK SONG

BÉLA BARTÓK (1881-1945)
from For Children
Transcribed by JERRY SNYDER

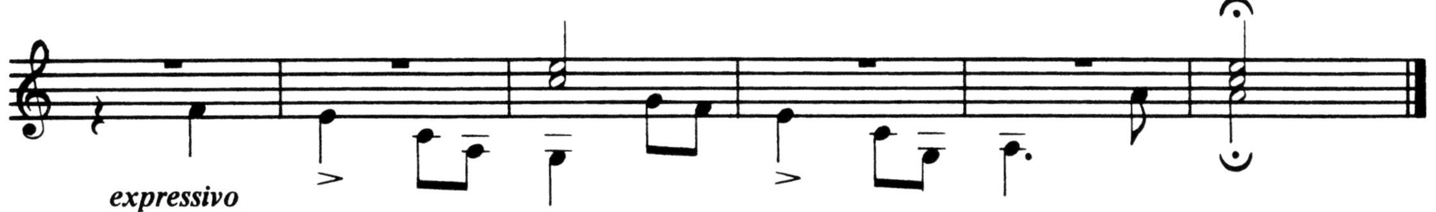

WALTZ

BÉLA BARTÓK (1881-1945)
from The First Term At The Piano
Transcribed by JERRY SNYDER

Tempo di Valse

mp

B II

mp

FUNERAL DIRGE

BÉLA BARTÓK (1881-1945)
from For Children
Transcribed by JERRY SNYDER

MINUET

BÉLA BARTÓK (1881-1945)
from The First Term At The Piano
Transcribed by JERRY SNYDER

MODERATO

BÉLA BARTÓK (1881-1945)
from Bartók-Reschofsky "Piano Method"
Transcribed by JERRY SNYDER

POCO VIVACE

BÉLA BARTÓK (1881-1945)
from For Children
Transcribed by JERRY SNYDER

ROUND

BÉLA BARTÓK (1881-1945)
from For Children
Transcribed by JERRY SNYDER

PLAY SONG

BÉLA BARTÓK (1881-1945)
from For Children
Transcribed by JERRY SNYDER

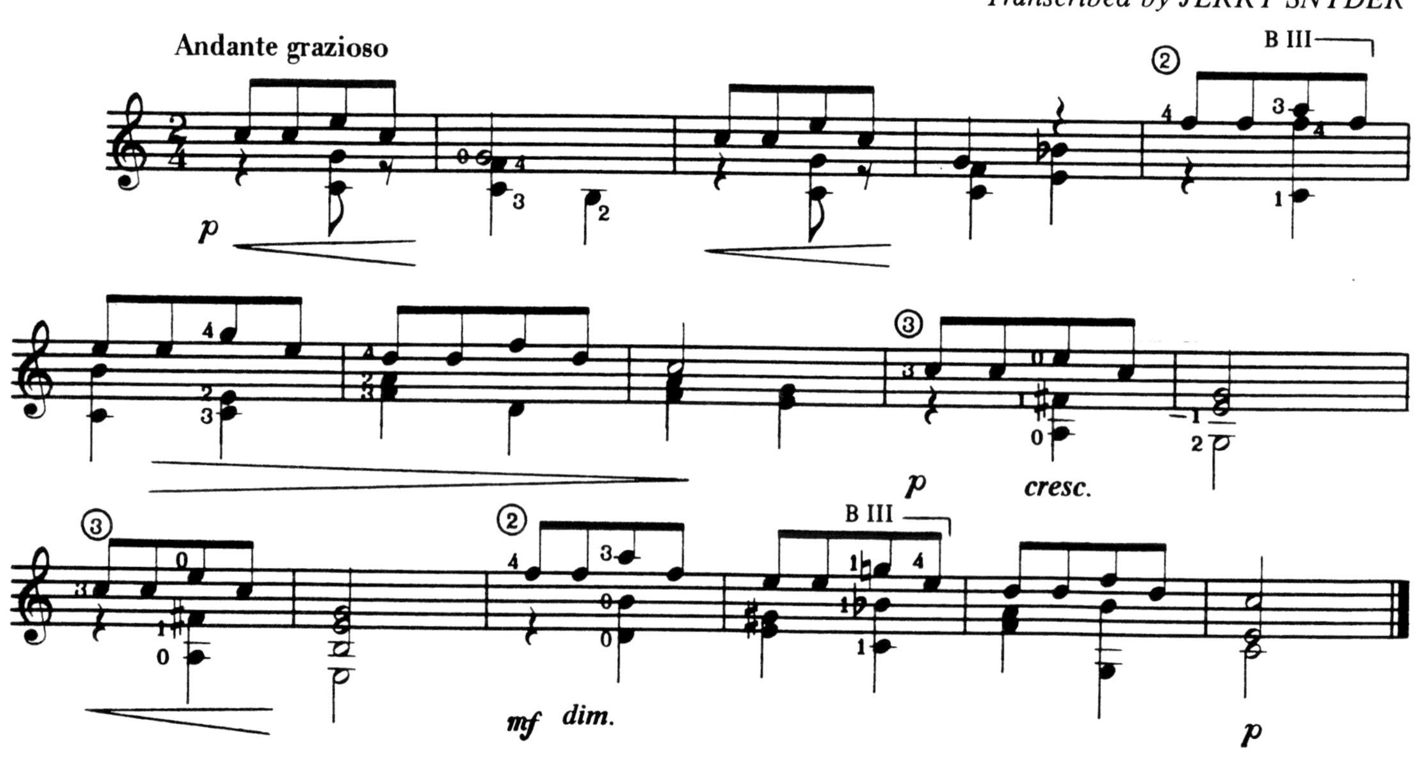

SONG

BÉLA BARTÓK (1881-1945)
From For Children
Transcribed by JERRY SNYDER

VARIATIONS

BÉLA BARTÓK (1881-1945)
from For Children
Transcribed by JERRY SNYDER

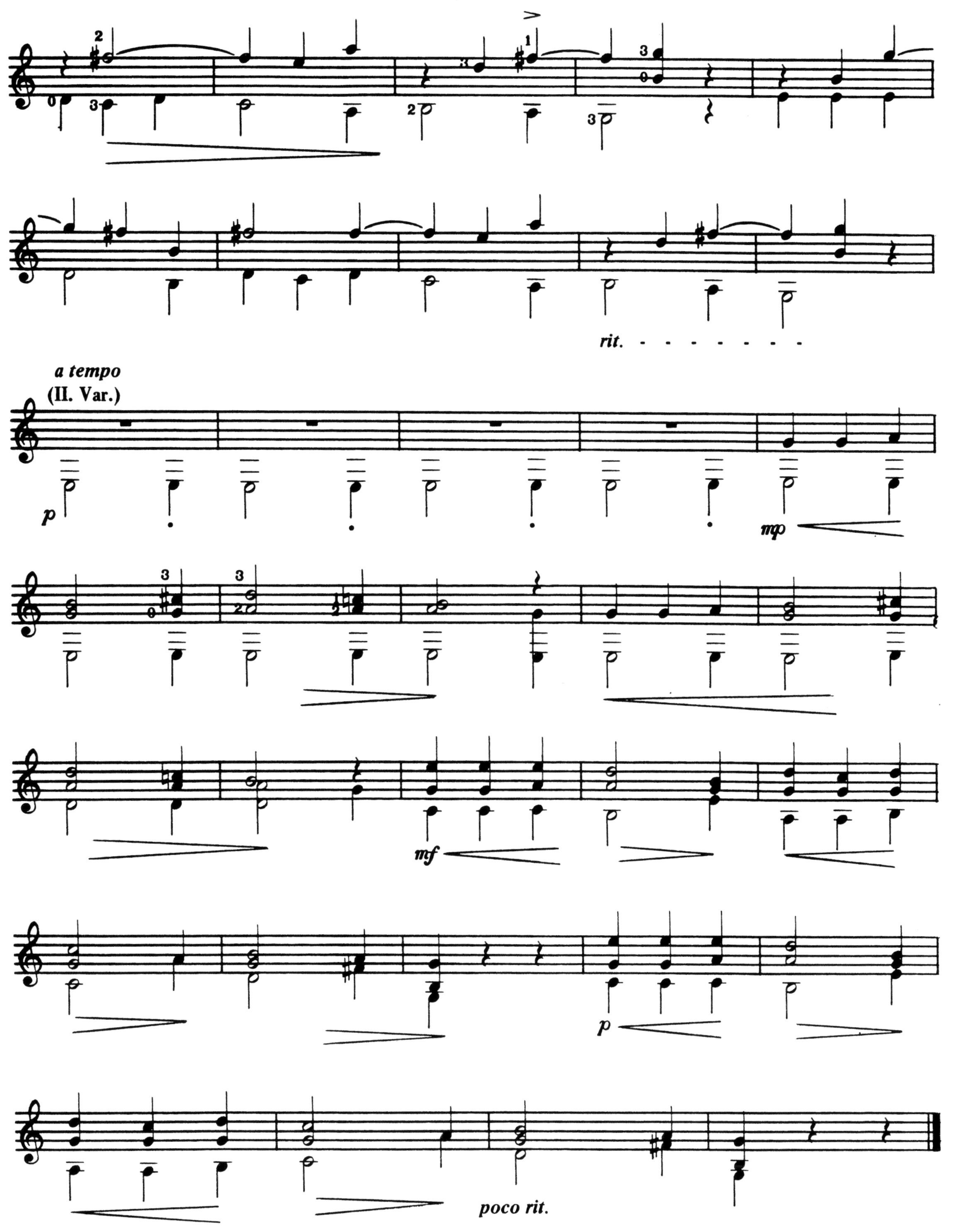
rit.
a tempo
(II. Var.)
p
mp
mf
p
poco rit.

ALLEMANDE and TRIO

LUDWIG VAN BEETHOVEN (1770-1827)
Wo O 42 Original in G
Transcribed by JERRY SNYDER

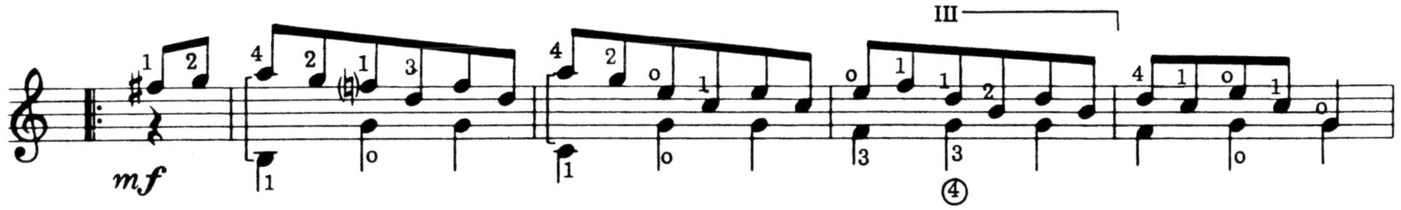

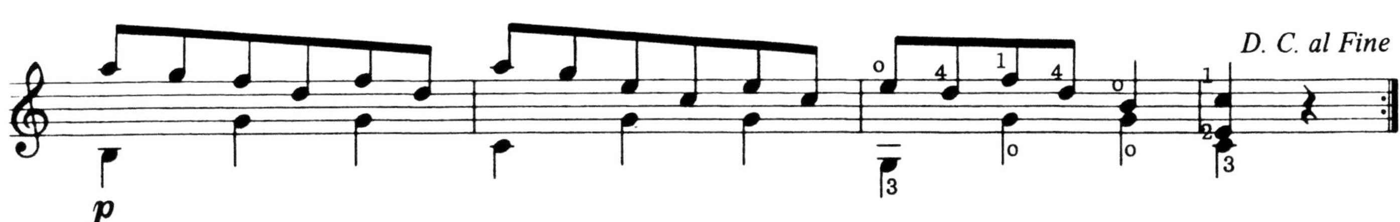

GERMAN DANCE

LUDWIG VAN BEETHOVEN (1770-1827)
Wo O 42
Transcribed by JERRY SNYDER

Allegretto

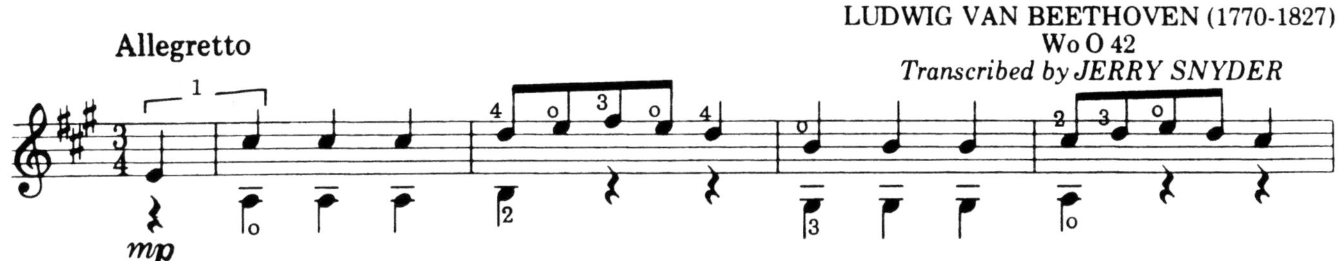

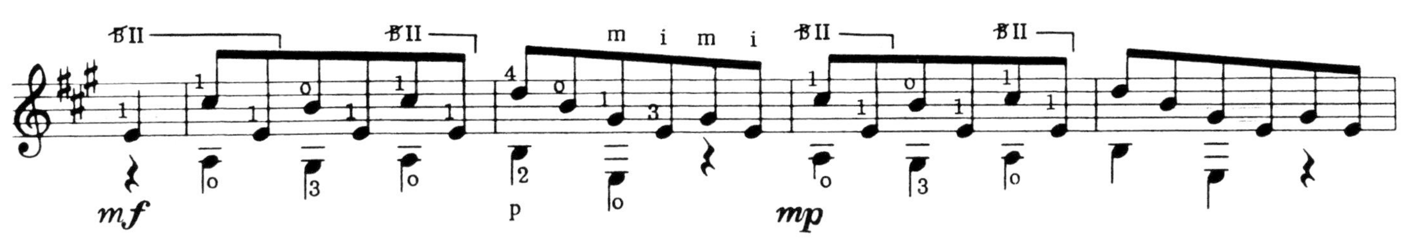

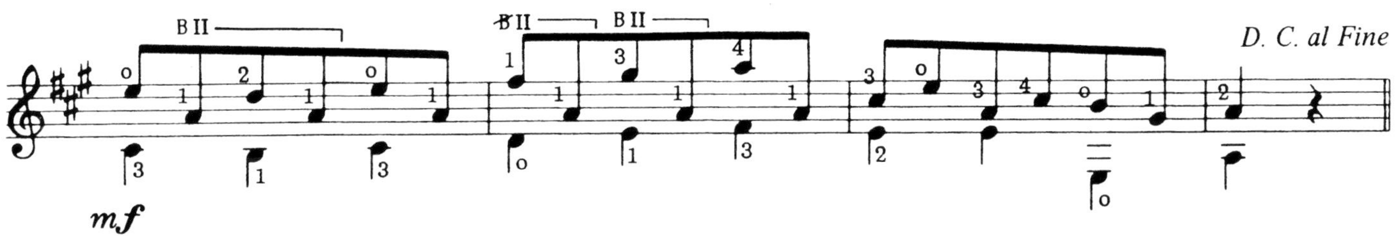

ECOSSAISE IN G

Ecossaise (the French word for Scottish) is the name given to short, country-type pieces in 2/4 time, composed by Beethoven, Schubert and others in the early 19th Century. Its origin is doubtful, particularly since there is no resemblance to any Scottish original. The Ecossaise is most likely a variant of a Scottish dance which evolved in Parisian ballrooms.

LUDWIG VAN BEETHOVEN (1770-1827)
Transcribed by JERRY SNYDER

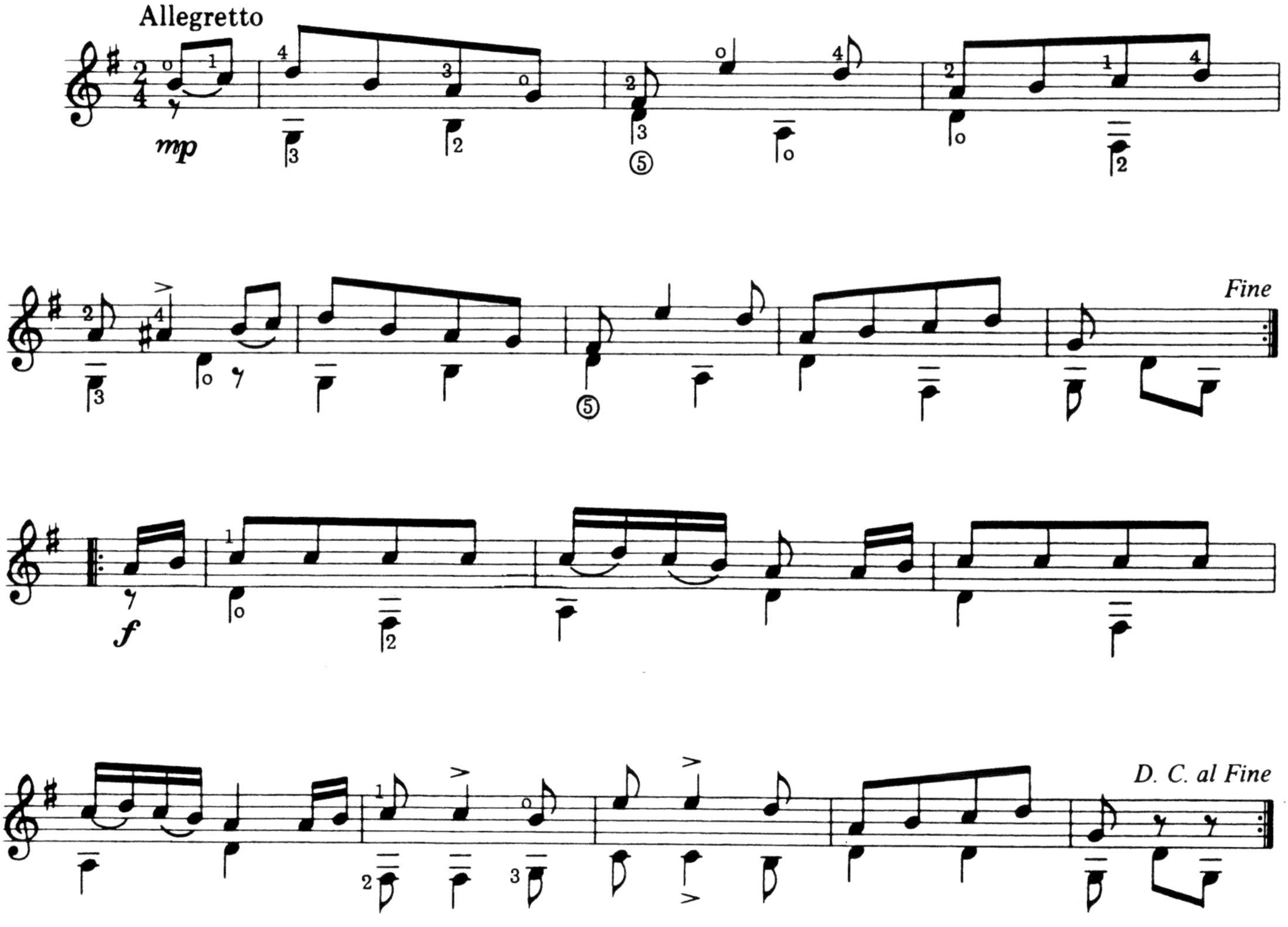
Allegretto
mp
Fine
f
D. C. al Fine

MINUET

LUDWIG VAN BEETHOVE (1770-1827)
(1796) Original in G
Transcribed by JERRY SNYDER

Allegretto
p
f
mf

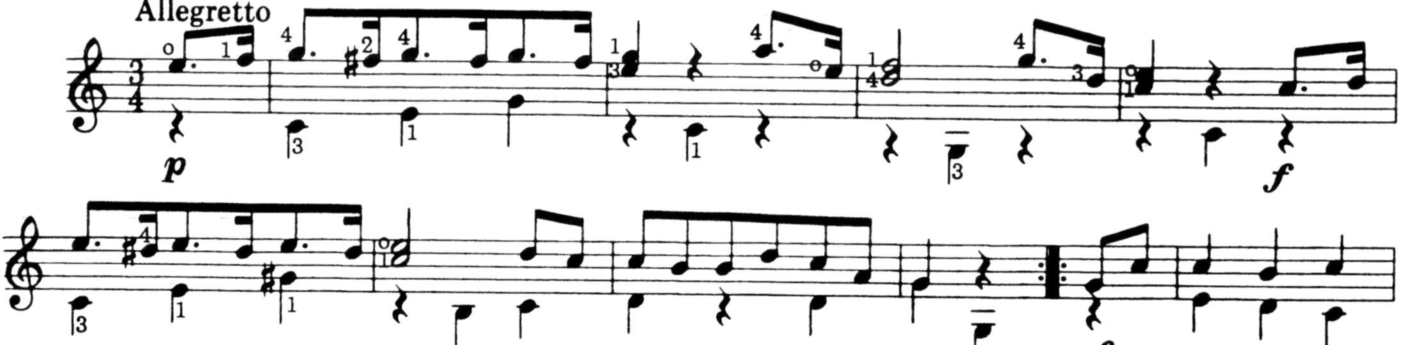

sf *f*

TRIO *Fine*

p

mf

p

D. C. al Fine

ODE TO JOY

Finale of Symphony No. 9 in D minor

LUDWIG VAN BEETHOVEN
Op. 125 (1817-1823) Original in D
Transcribed by JERRY SNYDER

Allegro assai

p

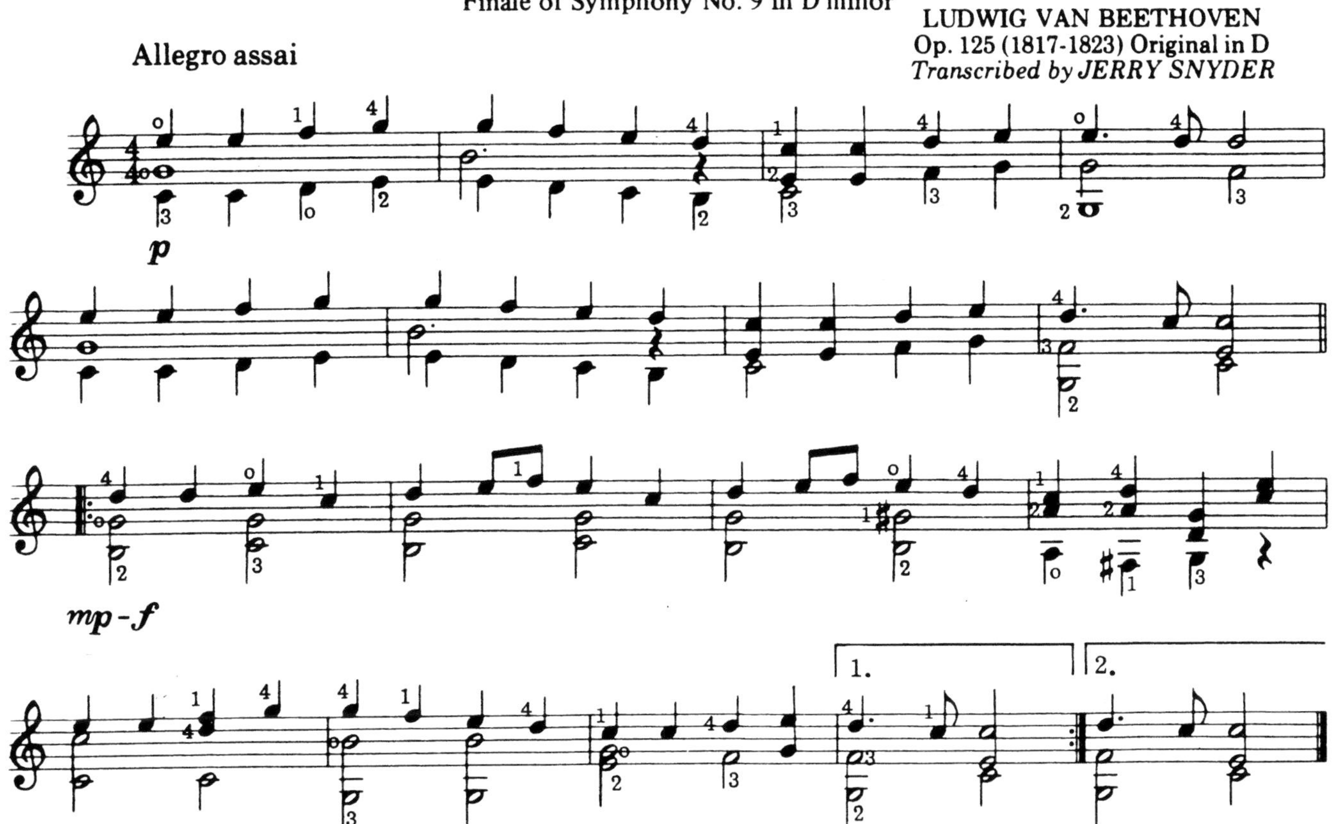

RONDOLETTO

LUDWIG VAN BEETHOVEN (1770-1827)
Transcribed by JERRY SNYDER

* The time signature has been changed to $\frac{3}{4}$ from the original $\frac{3}{8}$ in order to make the note values easier to read.

a tempo
p

f
p

cresc.
f

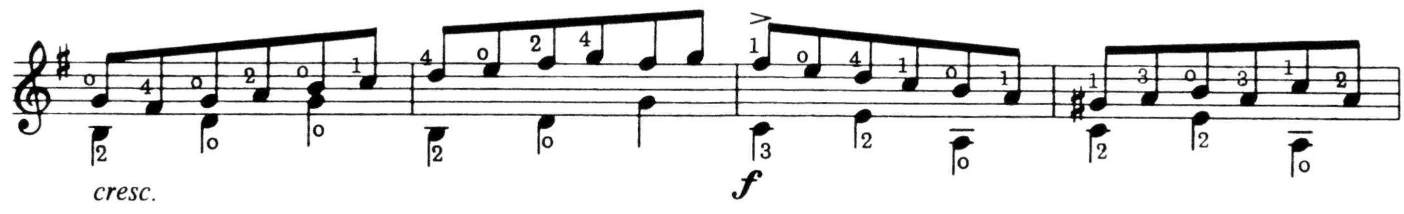
cresc.
f

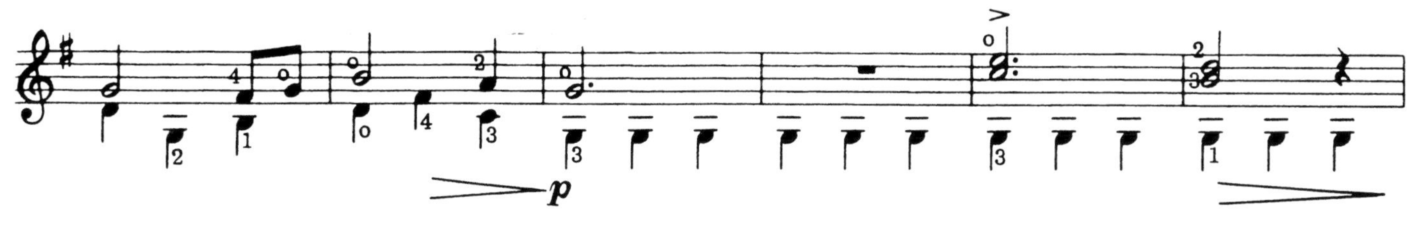
p

dim.
pp

MINUET

LUDWIG VAN BEETHOVE (1770-1827)
(1796) Original in G
Transcribed by JERRY SNYDER

CONTRE-DANCE

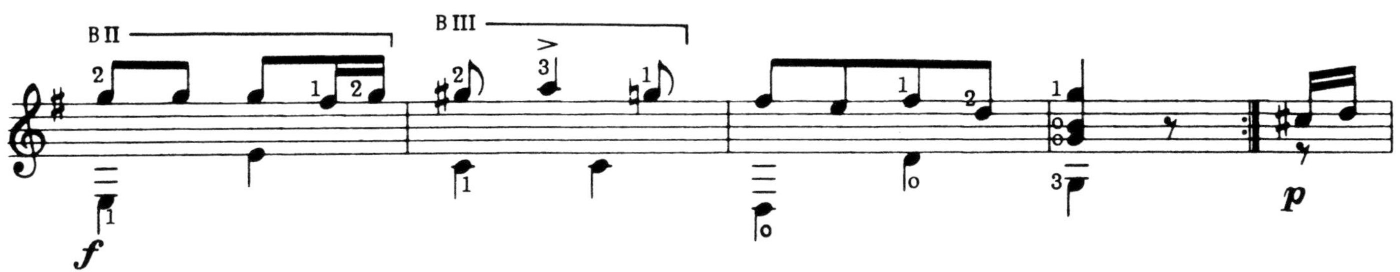

SONATINA IN G

LUDWIG VAN BEETHOVEN (1770-1827)
(Posthumous)
Transcribed by JERRY SNYDER

ROMANZE

LUDWIG VAN BEETHOVEN (1770-1827)
Original in G
Transcribed by JERRY SNYDER

Moderato

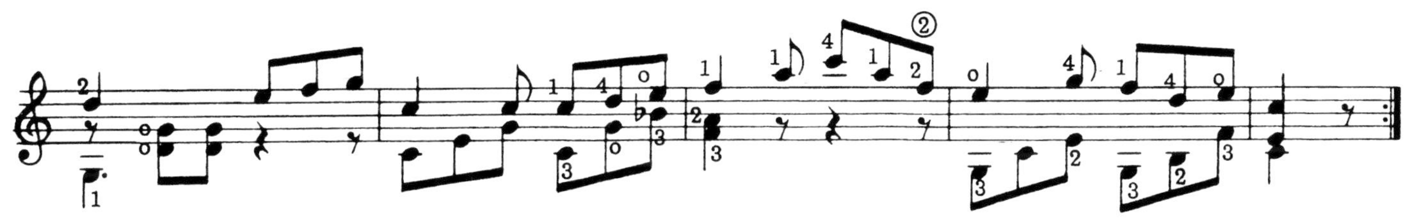

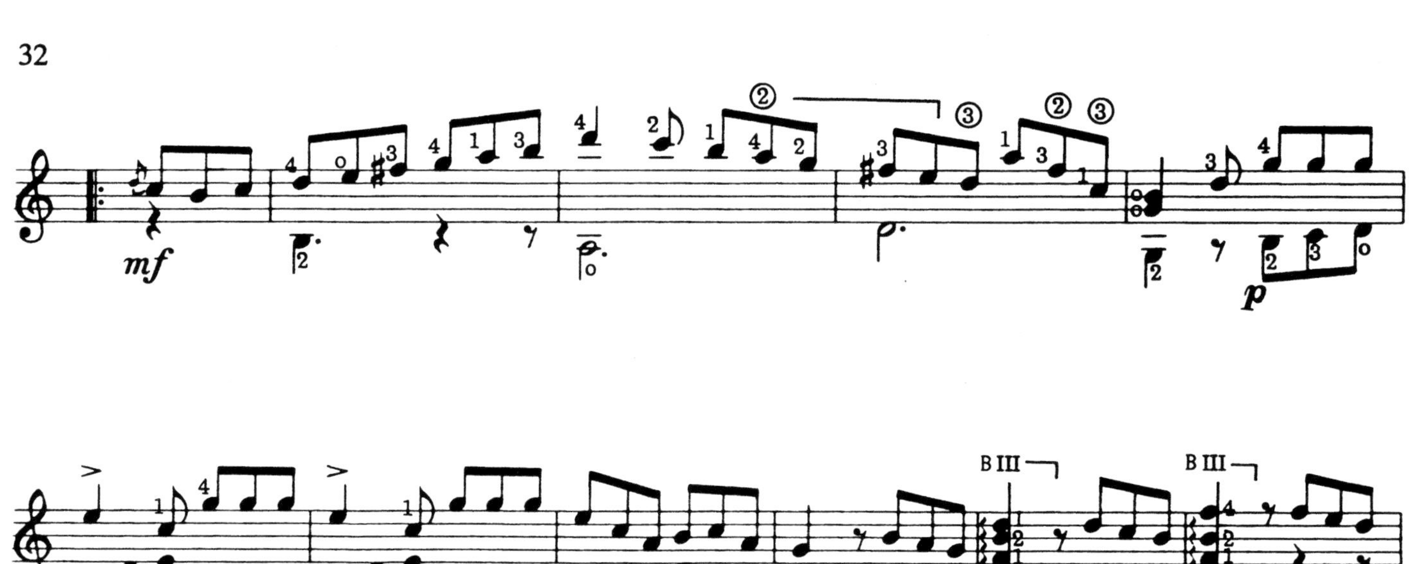
mf
p

B III
B III
cresc.

B III
a tempo
dim. e rit.
mp

cresc.

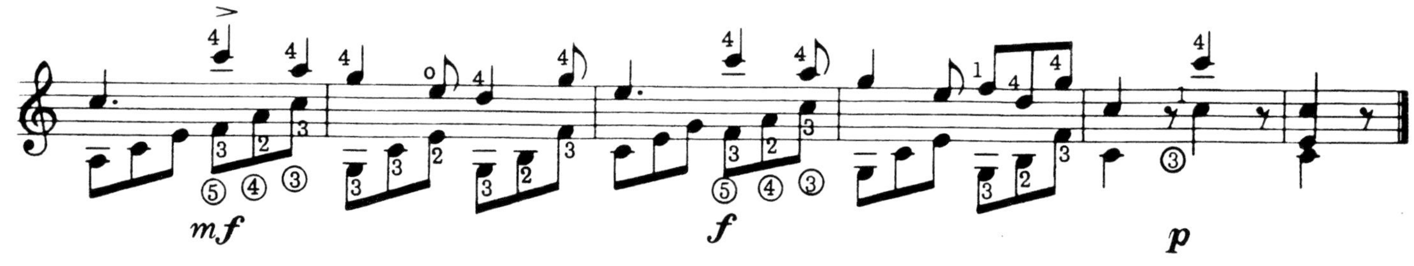
mf
f
p

RUSSIAN FOLK SONG

LUDWIG VAN BEETHOVEN (1770-1827)
Transcribed by JERRY SNYDER

Theme from

FÜR ELISE

LUDWIG VAN BEETHOVEN (1770-1827)
Original in C major (1810)
Transcribed by JERRY SNYDER

* The time signature has been changed to $\frac{3}{4}$ from the original $\frac{3}{8}$ in order to make the note values easier to read.

BOURRÉE

GEORGE FRIDERIC HANDEL (1685-1759
from the Flute Sonata in G major
Transcribed by JERRY SNYDER

AIR

GEORGE FRIDERIC HANDEL (1685-1759)
from the "Aylesford" manuscripts (Original in B♭ major)
Transcribed by JERRY SNYDER

Original in 3/8

IMPERTINENCE

GEORGE FRIDERIC HANDEL (1685-1759)
from the "Aylesford" manuscripts (Original in G minor)
Transcribed by JERRY SNYDER

GAVOTTE and VARIATION

GEORGE FRIDERIC HANDEL (1685-1759)
from Suite of Pieces pour le Clavecin
Transcribed by JERRY SNYDER

Variation

GAVOTTE

GEORGE FRIDERIC HANDEL (1685-1759)
from the "Aylesford" manuscripts
Transcribed by JERRY SNYDER

MINUET

GEORGE FRIDERIC HANDEL (1685-1759)
from the "Aylesford" manuscripts (Original in A minor)
Transcribed by JERRY SNYDER

MINUET

GEORGE FRIDERIC HANDEL (1685-1759)
from Courante e Due Menuetti
Transcribed by JERRY SNYDER

SARABANDE

GEORGE FRIDERIC HANDEL (1685-1759)
from the Harpsichord Suite in D minor
Transcribed by JERRY SNYDER

⑥– D

BIII

PASSEPIED

GEORGE FRIDERIC HANDEL (1685-1759)
from the "Aylesford" manuscripts
Transcribed by JERRY SNYDER

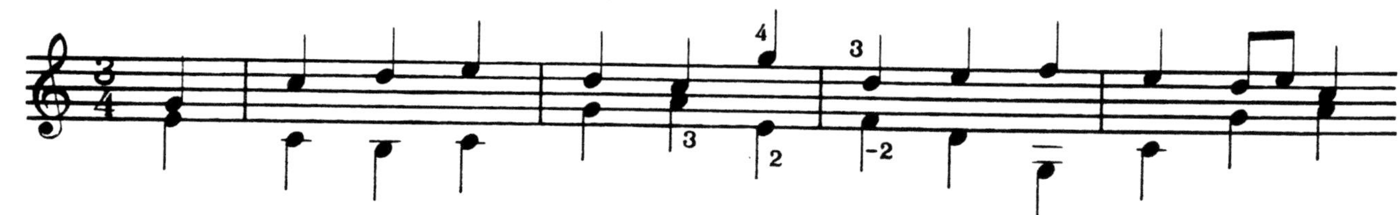

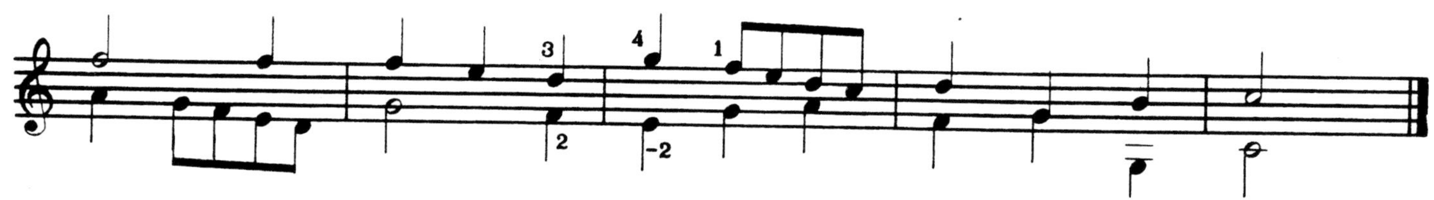

MINUET

GEORGE FRIDERIC HANDEL (1685-1759)
from the "Aylesford" manuscripts (Original in D minor)
Transcribed by JERRY SNYDER

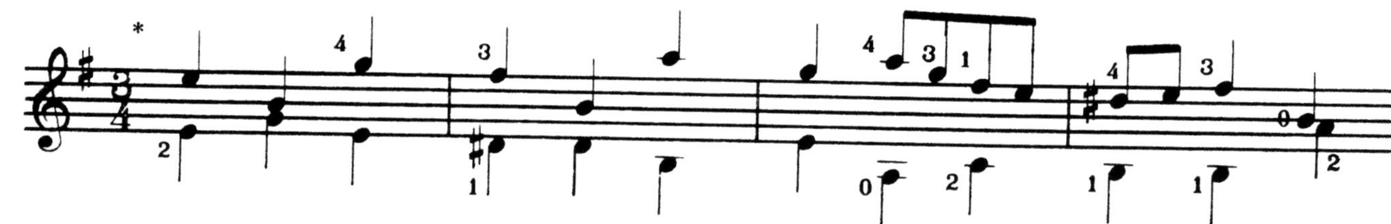

* Original in 3/8

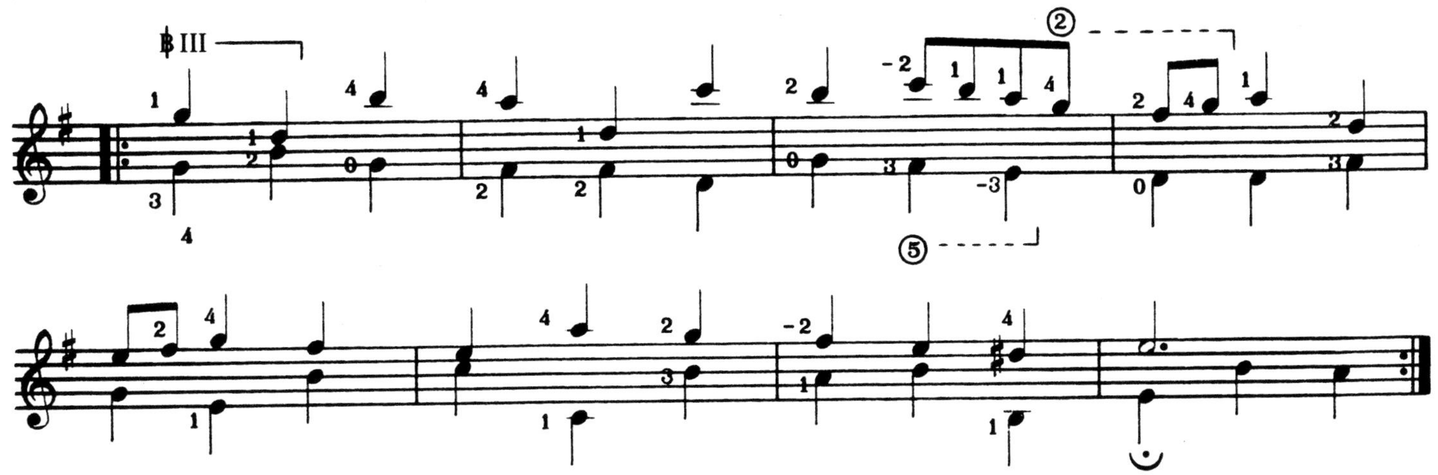

THE HARMONIOUS BLACKSMITH

GEORGE FRIDERIC HANDEL (1685-1759)
from the Harpsichord Suite V (Original in E major)
Transcribed by JERRY SNYDER

[Andantino]

* Original in 4/4

SARABANDE and VARIATIONS

GEORGE FRIDERIC HANDEL (1685-1759)
from the Harpsichord Suite in D minor
Transcribed by JERRY SNYDER

Variation II

SUITE FOR A MUSICAL CLOCK

GEORGE FRIDERIC HANDEL (1685-1759)
from the "Aylesford" manuscripts
Transcribed by JERRY SNYDER

Prelude

Minuet

Air

ALLEGRO

WOLFGANG AMADEUS MOZART (1756-1791)
K. 3 1762 (Age 6) Original in B♭
Transcribed by JERRY SNYDER

ANDANTE

WOLFGANG AMADEUS MOZART (1756-1791)
K. 15 mm (1764 or 1765) Original in E♭
Transcribed by JERRY SNYDER

MINUET

WOLFGANG AMADEUS MOZART (1756-1791)
K. 2 1762 (Age 6) Original in F
Transcribed by JERRY SNYDER

MINUET IN F

WOLFGANG AMADEUS MOZART (1756-1791)
K. 5 (1762)
Transcribed by JERRY SNYDER

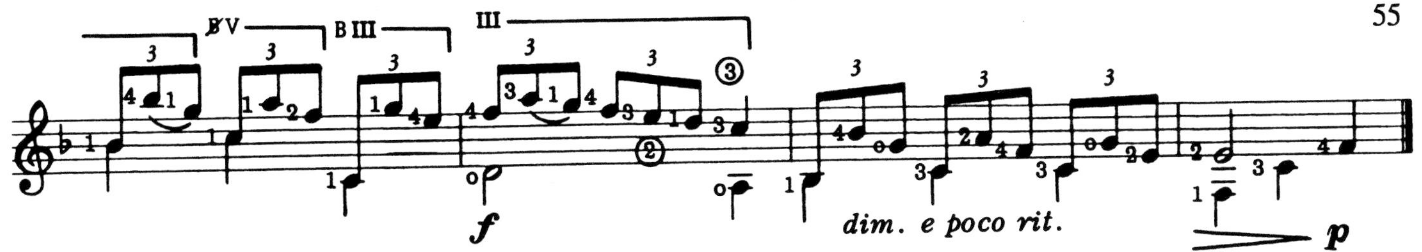

MINUET IN C

WOLFGANG AMADEUS MOZART (1756-1791)
K. 6 (1762)
Transcribed by JERRY SNYDER

Allegretto

MINUET No. 1

WOLFGANG AMADEUS MOZART (1756-1791)
K. 1 (1761 or 1762)
Transcribed by JERRY SNYDER

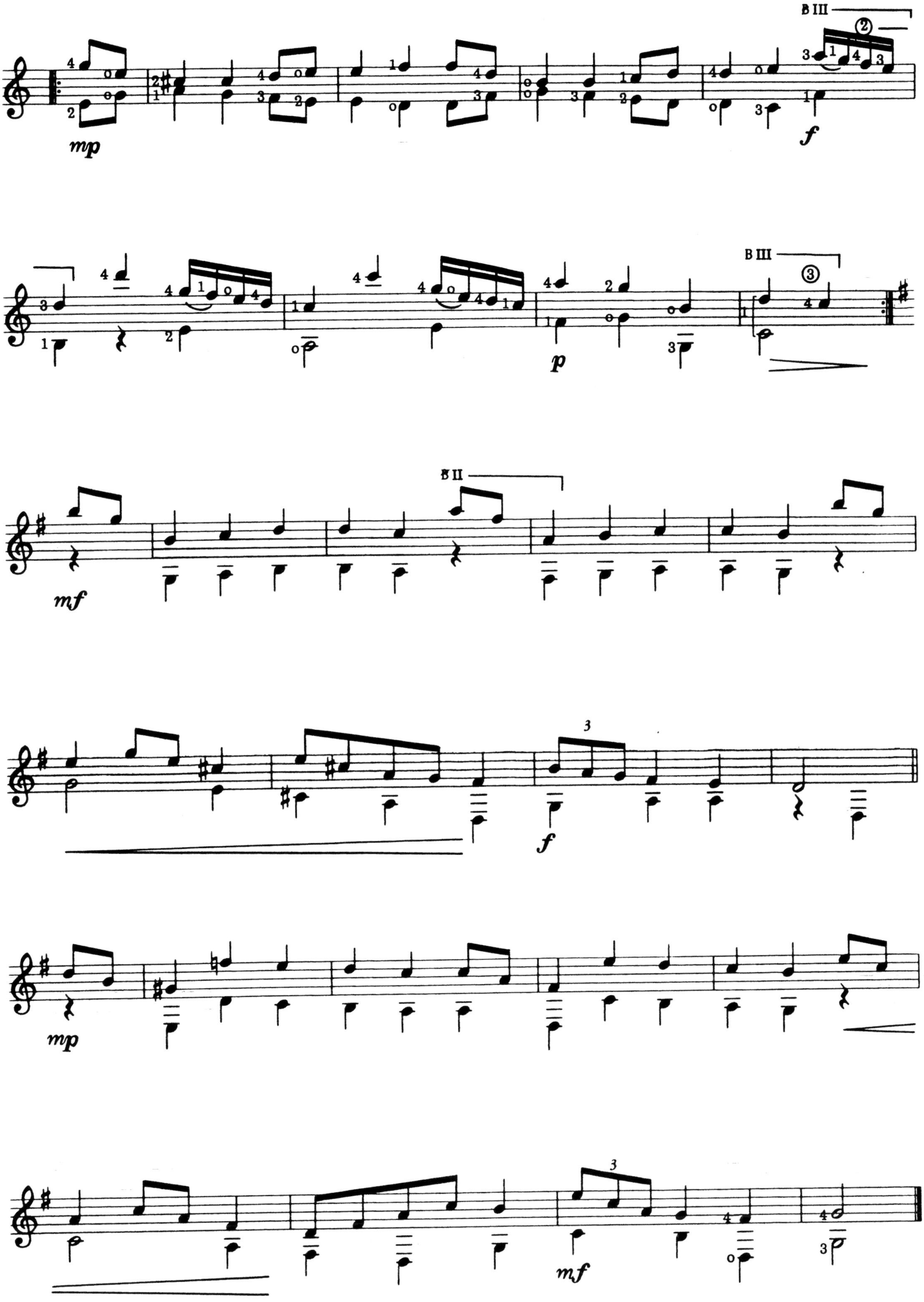
B III
mp
f
B III
p
B II
mf
f
mp
mf

MINUET

WOLFGANG AMADEUS MOZART (1756-1791)
Transcribed by JERRY SNYDER

MINUET
from Finale, Act I
"DON GIOVANNI" (Don Juan)

'Don Giovanni' is Mozart's operatic version of the old Spanish 'Don Juan' legend, which tells how a young nobleman, famous everywhere as a pursuer of women, finally meets his end. In a graveyard, Don Giovanni mocks the statue of the father of one of the women he has wronged, and invites him to supper. The statue appears, seizes Don Giovanni, and consigns him to Hell.

WOLFGANG AMADEUS MOZART K. 527 (1787)
Transcribed for guitar
by JERRY SNYDER

MINUET
EINE KLEINE NACHTMUSIK

WOLFGANG AMADEUS MOZART (1756-17
K.-V. 525 Original in G
Transcribed by JERRY SNYDER

mp
D.C. al Fine

Trio from the Menuetto

SYMPHONY No. 39

WOLFGANG AMADEUS MOZART (1756-1791)
K.-V. 543 (1788) Original in E♭
Transcribed by JERRY SNYDER

Theme from 1st Movement

SYMPHONY No. 40

WOLFGANG AMADEUS MOZART (1756-1791)
K. 550 (1778) Original in G minor
Transcribed by JERRY SNYDER

THEME FOR VARIATION

from Sonata in A

'Theme and Variations' is one of the oldest of musical forms, indicating a tune followed by varied versions of it. In many examples, the harmonic basis remains the same throughout, while the melody is continually changed. In others, the harmony changes but the melody clings to some semblance of the original tune.

WOLFGANG AMADEUS MOZART (1756-1791)
K. 331 (1779) Original in A
Transcribed by JERRY SNYDER

First Movement from

VIENNESE SONATINA IV

WOLFGANG AMADEUS MOZART (1756-1791)
K. 439b (1783) Original in B♭
Transcribed by JERRY SNYDER

GAVOTTE

DOMENICO SCARLATTI (1685-1757)
(Original in D minor) K. 64; L. 58
Transcribed by JERRY SNYDER

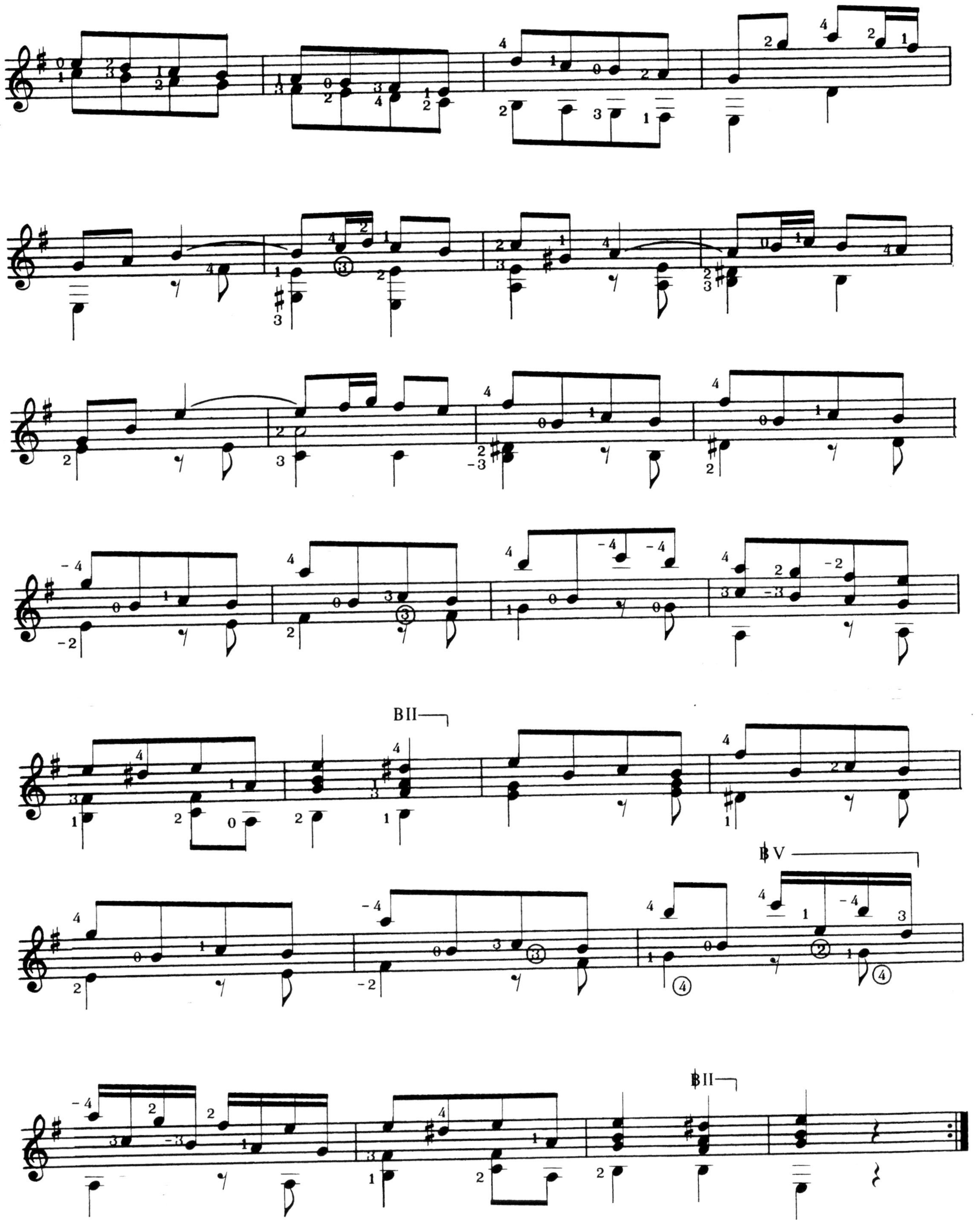
BII
BV
BII

LARGHETTO

DOMENICO SCARLATTI (1685-1757)
K. 34; L.S. 7
Transcribed by JERRY SNYDER

MINUET

DOMENICO SCARLATTI (1685-1757)
(Original in C minor) K. 73c; L. 217
Transcribed by JERRY SNYDER

III — III — V — ₵I — VII — BIII — ₵II — D. C.

* Original in 3/8

ARIA

DOMENICO SCARLATTI (1685-1757)
(Original in D minor) K. 32; L. 423
Transcribed by JERRY SNYDER

Allegro

* Original in 3/8

MINUET

DOMENICO SCARLATTI (1685-1757)
(Original in G minor) K. 88; L. 36
Transcribed by JERRY SNYDER

* Original in 3/8

MINUET

DOMENICO SCARLATTI (1685-1757)
(Original in B♭) K. 42; L. S. 36
Transcribed by JERRY SNYDER

MINUET

DOMENICO SCARLATTI (1685-1757)
K. 73b; L. 217
Transcribed by JERRY SNYDER

* Original in 3/8

PASTORALE

DOMENICO SCARLATTI (1685-1757)
(Original in D) K. 415; L.S. 11
Transcribed by JERRY SNYDER

Allegro

BIII
BIII

SONATA

DOMENICO SCARLATTI (1685-1757)
K. 90d; L. 106
Transcribed by JERRY SNYDER

* Original in 3/8

MINUET

DOMENICO SCARLATTI (1685-1757)
(Original in F) K. 78; L. 75
Transcribed by JERRY SNYDER

* Original in 3/8

SONATA

DOMENICO SCARLATTI (1685-1757)
K. 322; L. 483
Transcribed by JERRY SNYDER

Allegro

BII
BIII
BII
BI
1.
2.
IX
BIX
BVII

BV
BII
BIII
BIII
BVII
BII
BII